IMAGES
of America

ELGIN

ILLINOIS
FROM THE COLLECTION OF
THE ELGIN AREA HISTORICAL SOCIETY

This is a group of Elgin pioneers, pictured in 1866.

IMAGES
of America

ELGIN

ILLINOIS

FROM THE COLLECTION OF
THE ELGIN AREA HISTORICAL SOCIETY

Jim and Wynette Edwards

ARCADIA
PUBLISHING

Published by Arcadia Publishing
Charleston, South Carolina

Library of Congress Catalog Card Number: 2007922634

For all general information contact Arcadia Publishing at:
Telephone 843-853-2070
Fax 843-853-0044
E-mail sales@arcadiapublishing.com
For customer service and orders:
Toll-Free 1-888-313-2665

Visit us on the Internet at www.arcadiapublishing.com

Left: James Gifford wanted to establish a town on the Fox River, and his brother Hezekiah wanted to farm the area that they founded in 1835. James became the first Elgin postmaster, beginning in 1837.
These portraits of James Gifford and his wife, Laura Raymond Gifford (*Right*), are attributed to Sheldon Peck, internationally recognized portrait artist of the early to mid-1800s. The two portraits now hang in the Elgin Area Historical Museum. (JME.)

CONTENTS

ACKNOWLEDGMENTS

Elgin has been fortunate to have had so many excellent historians, photographers, and collectors over the years. We are deeply indebted to Elmer Gylleck, Howard Gusler, and Galen Williams, who collected stories or photographed Elgin as it was growing up. Thanks go out to them and to the many others who gave personal photographs and other memorabilia to the Elgin Area Historical Society.

Those who wrote of Elgin's history—Waite and Frank Joslyn, Hazel Belle Perry, and E.C. Alft—have provided a wealth of information from eyewitness accounts over the years. Alft is still Elgin's reigning historian at the millennium. The people of Elgin are very fortunate to have such a good writer who also is so deeply interested in the city's goings-on.

This book would not have been possible without the cooperation of the Elgin Area Historical Museum and its director, Elizabeth Marston. Many thanks go to Carl Flaks, Rachael Campbell, Marge Rowe, Becky Minetti, and Sara Ellen Anderson, who helped pull pictures and spent hours providing indexing and proofreading skills. Such volunteers are the life-blood of a good museum.

Almost all of the photographs in this book are from the Elgin Area Historical Society. There are a few, however, from the author's collection. These are marked after the caption with "(JME.)."

This Greek Revival building, constructed in 1856, came to be called, "Old Main." Now the museum for the Elgin Area Historical Society, it was first used by Elgin Academy, a private school chartered in 1839. Elgin Academy is still located on this same hill.

INTRODUCTION

Elgin is called the "tick tock" town. The town made famous all over the world for its precision pocket watches is much more than just watches. Conservators of Elgin's history, who have kept the past of the city alive by collecting photographs, documents, and other artifacts, will tell you that there are thousands of other stories to be told about this major American city, whose products made their way into Europe, Asia, and other distant parts of the globe at the turn of the 20th century. This volume, which is a pictorial narrative, selectively picks many rare, never-before-published photographs of the people of Elgin, as well as their houses, businesses, and passionate interests, from the city's beginning through the first part of the 1930s. Beginning with chapter two and continuing with the start of each chapter, panoramic scenes of the city of Elgin show the changing look of the downtown area.

Music has played a part in the life of the Elgin community from its very beginning. The immigrants to this great city came from all over the globe by the 20th century, but the "German culture connection" was especially strong before the start of the 1900s. Early German and Yankee settlers brought their love of music with them to their new home. Soon the arts were flourishing in local opera houses, and parks came alive with the music of the watch company's band and its famous conductor. In the late 1800s, one could attend various club and society meetings, held regularly and dedicated to the study of music and literature. Men and women had the opportunity to study painting or dance or to visit the famous Gail Borden Public Library, rated as one of the best libraries in the state from its beginning.

Elgin was strategically located close to its big brother, Chicago, to the east and was on the way to Galena to the west. The river supplied water for manufacturers, and the railroad supplied the means to transport goods to market. The city became a trade center for upper Illinois farmers and businessmen. When Elgin hit its first big boom after the Civil War and into the 1870s, the city had such a large number and variety of merchants that it became almost a world unto itself. At this time, the Elgin Watch factory, State Asylum, Elgin Academy, public schools, and Borden Milk Company were part of the ever expanding cityscape. Gas came to town in 1871, and people discarded their candles and lamps. They also discarded a past, more tranquil life style and set about creating a better environment for working, leisure-time activities, culture, and family activities. Elgin was full of pride and ingenuity and willing to reinvent itself when called upon to do so. It still is today.

August Scheele sits proudly in his grocery store in this photograph taken in 1900. He and others emigrated from that part of Germany that was once the kingdom of Hanover before 1871. He began his grocer career by clerking in a general store but opened his own store in 1899. Scheele made it a point to be the one who opened the store each day, always looking at the store from the viewpoint of the customer. As you can see from the window placement, this first store was in a basement, but a new store building was completed in 1902 and expanded in 1910.

One

THE GOOD OLD HORSE AND BUGGY DAYS

The first settlers/builders of Elgin saw the land as it had been, was, and might be in the future. These sentiments were perfectly captured by a poem called "The Pioneers."

> There were builders back in the long ago
> Who lived in their house of dreams.
> There were visions of traffic along the fair hills
> And of power that lay in the streams.
> Then the river was curbed in its wayward course
> By hands that were strong and firm,
> Till its wasted force was harnessed fast
> And the wheels began to turn.
> They dreamed of the Indian trails far down
> 'Neath the pavement of city streets.
> They saw the red campfire's glow disappear
> In the light of the forge's white heat;
> They had visions there of the future years
> When the work of the day was done,
> When a path of gold was blazed in the west
> By the chariot of the sun.
> So the motor's hum and the whirring wheels
> In the busy marts of trade,
> The flying sparks, the anvil's ring
> Where the rails of steel are laid;
> The rolling smoke from the shops and mills
> That are famous far and near.
> Industry, commerce and progress today
> Were the dreams of the pioneer.

Underneath the Utopian picture that this poet paints of the early pioneers is the reality that, along the way, there was some stumbling. From the later half of the 1900s and into the next century, the city would experience a period of natural and man-made disasters, racial and ethnic conflicts, and some years of economic downturns.

But, by Elgin's centennial year, 1936, the city had lived up to many of the dreams of its early settlers, having grown to a population of some 40,000 citizens. That year, the city hosted ten conventions. The highlight of the celebration during Industrial Week was the cutting up of a huge, 500-pound Elgin birthday cake made by the bakers of the city. Lucky bystanders got pieces of the cake, which might contain an Elgin watch or some other Elgin product.

Livery owners operated much as taxi owners do today. They did not wait for people to come to them, but instead met them at the depots, hotels, and on the streets. They took pride in their fine horses, well-maintained carriages, and courteous and speedy service.

Frank Gould is seated on the bench outside the boathouse of his livery. Gould's Boat Livery was located on the west bank of the Fox River at the foot of Oak Street. Later this property was also the location of The Structural Steel Co., then the Elgin Tower & Tank Co., and finally the Elgin Street Sweeper Co.

Blacksmiths were essential craftsmen in early Elgin. Jason House, G.W. Renwick, and Samuel Hunting were the first permanent ones. Blacksmiths not only shod horses, but did general blacksmithing such as hinge making and repair work. Pictured here is Peter Gruer in his shop near the turn of the 20th century. The other men are not identified.

This was an early ad for A.F. Curtis, an Elgin tinner. The photograph was taken on River Side Drive looking north at Chicago Street. Curtis practiced the tinsmith trade on and off from 1884 to 1911. He also tried his hand at shoemaking and watch making.

Keeping chickens in the back yard was common in villages such as Elgin throughout the 1800s and the early 1900s. This is Muriel Fraser in her backyard on Division Street with the family's source of eggs, "cookie jar money," and Sunday dinner. Houses were not close together, and the outhouse was always as far away from the main house as possible.

Historian Elmer Gylleck noted that this picture is of a farmer taking his milk to town to be processed. It was taken on the northwest side of Elgin before 1910. This was a common sight in Elgin throughout the 1800s and early 1900s, when milk was a major industry.

The center of downtown Elgin was a very busy place in the 1890s. Shops with awnings lined the streets, and banks anchored several blocks in the area. Beneath the second-floor office of a dentist was one of the city's first banks, the Elgin National Bank, organized in 1892. The fortress-like look of the facade of the bank lends a certain quality of solidness to the business. The lady with an umbrella in front of the bank appears as a black outline because of the intense sun that blocked all light to her features.

By 1902, the bank had eliminated the narrow windows and rough stonework and replaced them with wide, arched windows and doorways. New, smooth stone work was added. The original columns and porch banisters were kept, but the fancy eyebrows over the windows were changed to another design. About this time, trolleys and automobiles were rushing past the bank rather than horse-drawn carriages.

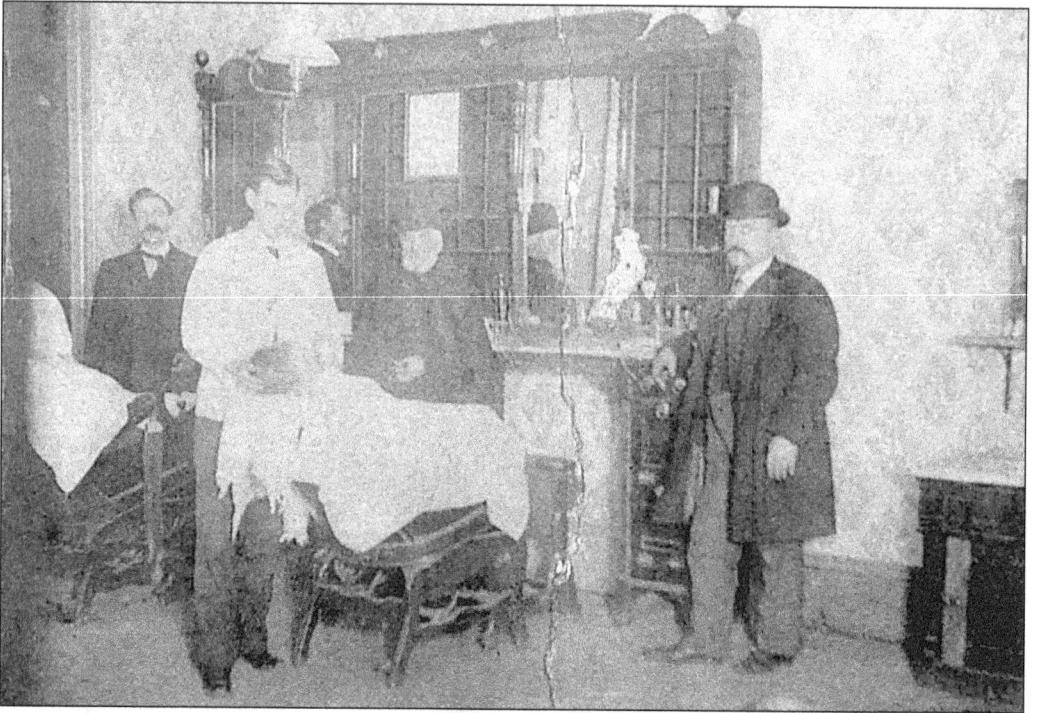

Barbershops were places where men shared the latest local news and gossip. Pictured here, in 1889, is Billy Bleier's Barber Shop, located on Douglas Avenue. Standing from left to right are as follows: Billy Bleier, Fred C. Dobler, Charles Wilkinson, and William Holden. The man receiving his shave is unknown.

Joseph Hemmens and Patrick Jones operated as tailors at 32-36 East Chicago Street from 1859 to about 1900. This photograph was taken sometime between 1875 and 1880. Hemmens and Jones were advertised as dealers in hats, caps, and gent's (men's) furnishing goods, with custom work in merchant tailoring a specialty.

Fountain Square was the market place of Elgin, but it was not a square. It was a triangle! This early fountain provided a place to water the horses after a long trip into town. The original town was platted 1 mile in each direction from the center of this fountain. Prior to the fountain being built in 1878, Fountain Square was called Market Square.

Streets were either dirt or mud through most of the 1800s. Paving was begun only in the late 1800s. This 1871 scene of Grove Avenue shows Payne Stable, Elgin Marble Works, and Baldwin Drugs. Wooden sidewalks were standard in the days of horses and buggies and long skirts, and they contributed to the fire hazard in a town.

Local craftsmen made custom-fitted shoes in Elgin in the early 1850s. The 1860 census shows more than 20 individual shoemakers in town. This 1897 picture of Chicago Shoe Store lists all those standing, except the one who wrote on the back. He listed himself as, "yours truly, first job at $2.50 per week." Identified are, from left to right, as follows: Newsome, Mark Meyer (owner), Gus Heldberg (shoe repair man), "yours truly," Phil Panemo (clerk), and Dick Connell (clerk).

Around 1900, Edward A. and Henry C. Leitner operated Leitner Bros. Meat Market and had a wagon that traveled through the neighborhood to sell meat. The butcher has his knife and steel in hand to cut the beef to order. The Leitner building is on the southeast corner of Spring and East Chicago Streets.

16

Some Elgin customers went to H.H. Volstorff Meat Market on River (now Grove) Street in 1888. The employers standing in the doorway are not identified, but the wares are on view for the purchaser. There were two Volstorff meat markets in Elgin for many years.

Albert Ansel's Market had a large variety of meats, including one spectacular turkey ready to be plucked, displayed for the Christmas season in 1900. Identified from left to right are Carrie Ansel, Carl Buehler, and Albert Ansel (on the far right). The sawdust on the floor concealed the blood dripping from the hanging meat.

Meierhoff & Rehage grocery store displayed their fresh produce outside to entice customers to shop in their store at 71 South Grove Avenue in the summer of 1904. Meierhoff operated his own grocery several years before Rehage joined him in this venture. Green grocers and butchers operated separate stores, and housewives visited each of them every day or so.

Paul G. Hagemann Grocery Store, at 562 Walnut, probably had an outside display as well. Notice the sausages in the case on the right side. The store is filled to the ceiling with canned goods, fresh produce, cheese, and sausage. The displays were cluttered and fully packed to give the impression of abundance. The first recorded grocer in Elgin was Phio S. Patterson.

Theodore F. Swan moved to Elgin in 1867. He was first a grocer, before expanding into dry goods. Around 1870, a large dry goods and grocery store was opened in the DuBois opera house block under the name of DuBois, Swan & Richards. Three years later, Swan bought out his partners' interests and operated the business alone. These women are shopping for corsets at Swan in the late 1800s.

By 1881, Swan was known as one of the most reliable dealers in the city. By 1914, the year this photograph was taken, women were purchasing more ready-to-wear clothing. In 1906, there were 50 dressmakers listed in the city directory. In 1907, there were only 20, but the number did go up in following years.

19

Shops were not always as specialized as they are now. F.A. Copeland, jeweler at 166 Chicago Street, sold typewriters and many musical items, as well as watches and jewelry. The first jeweler in the city was William Barker, who opened for business in 1845.

Nick Goedert Saloon is shown as it was in 1903, probably serving up beer made by the Eagle Brewery's owner, Casper Althen. Goedert opened this saloon on Chicago Street in 1884 and ran it until Elgin voted dry in 1914. Hezekiah Gifford opened the first tavern in 1836, but it sold no liquor.

20

Two

FATHER TIME, CHEESE, AND MR. BORDEN

The explosive growth of the milk industry in and around Elgin can be counted in the increase in cows. In 1855, there were 800 cows in the area with 1,000 pounds of cheese and 4,000 pounds of butter processed. By 1875, there were 13,000 cows in the same area with 2,000,000 pounds of cheese and 550,000 pounds of butter produced. As the products increased in quantity and quality, so did their reputation. Elgin butter and cheese were found in stores from San Francisco to New York and even in Liverpool. Besides producing the milk to manufacture these quantities, three carloads were sent to Chicago daily. When too many farmers were selling milk, butter, and cheese, the condensing factory took the surplus in its operation.

The Elgin National Watch Company had sales representatives in every civilized country, and it was advertised that its watches announced the time of day to nations "from Greenland's icy mountains to India's coral strands." Company stock was issued in 1865, but the first watch was not turned out until 1867. The first task of the new company was to build the facility and machines that would be needed to manufacture the watch parts. Up to this time, watches had been built individually, not in assembly production.

Elgin was just a small settlement in 1866, the year that this photograph was taken. Individual homes backed up to the river, with the outhouse as far away from the house as possible. Each yard was fenced to keep animals in place, but the barnyards were not generally fenced. You can see Monday's wash on the line in this view of the west bank.

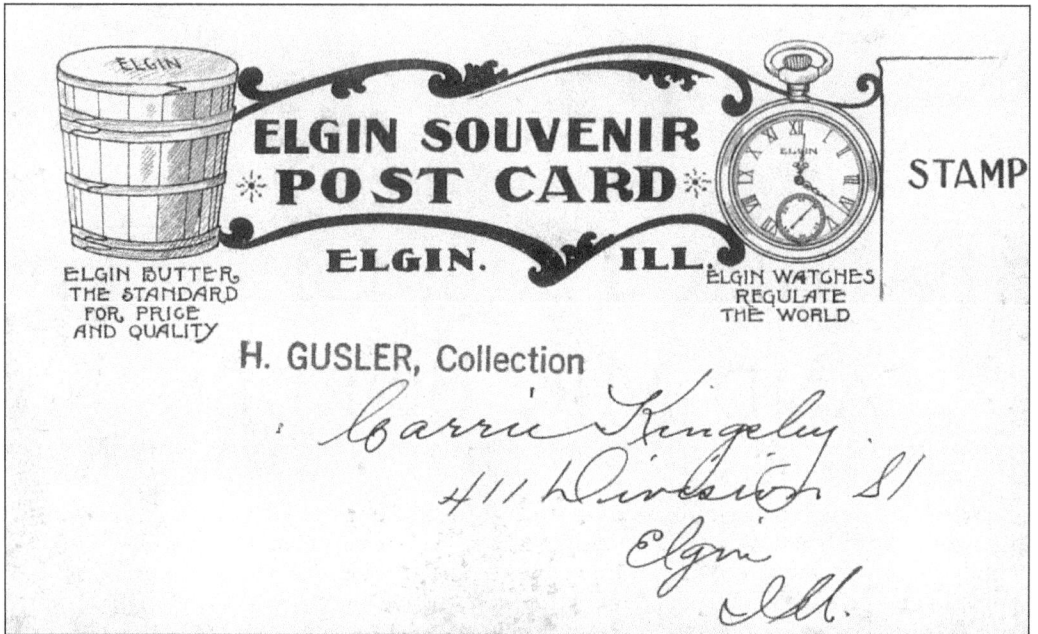

ELGIN SOUVENIR POST CARD ELGIN. ILL.

ELGIN

ELGIN BUTTER, THE STANDARD FOR PRICE AND QUALITY

ELGIN WATCHES REGULATE THE WORLD

STAMP

H. GUSLER, Collection

Carrie Kingely
411 Division St.
Elgin
Ill.

Milk products and watches were the first goods that took Elgin trade beyond the borders of Kane County. The 1904 *History of Kane County* recorded that Phineas H. Smith shipped the first can of milk sold out of the county to Chicago's "Adams House" via rail in 1852.

PRODUCERS OF ELGIN BUTTER

The first Kane County farmers produced crops that would yield quick returns to meet their immediate needs. During the first 15 or 20 years of the county's settlement, wheat was a staple crop. Early in the 1850s, the yield began to decline, and farmers turned to dairy farming.

Gail Borden perfected a method of canning condensed milk in 1858. This milk became a staple of the Union troops in the Civil War. When Borden needed more production space, he located a condensing plant in Elgin because of the strong dairy industry there. This 1908 photograph shows the wagons used to deliver milk all over Elgin.

Elgin Condensed Milk Co. was in business in 1867 at State and Highland. Twenty thousand quarts of rich, pure milk were processed each day by 1891. The company was purchased by Borden in February of 1894, increasing the size of Borden's Illinois Condensing Company.

Springbrook Creamery was one of the many creameries that began to promote the fact that their butter came from Elgin, Illinois. Springbrook Creamery operated 13 factories by 1891. Dairy products from Elgin were sought out, and prices were quoted in both domestic and foreign markets.

When Borden's company first arrived in Elgin, it employed 30 men and 26 women. By 1891, 250 were employed and 40,000 quarts of milk were being processed daily. Writers of the day wrote of the "excessive neatness and cleanliness" of the factory. This 1899 photograph shows some of the participants in the first annual Borden's picnic, at what is now Tyler Creek Forest Preserve.

As the milk business grew, increased attention was given to the developing of improved strains of milk-producing stock. Few of the dairymen seemed to have full-bred cows, but rather cross-bred Durham, Hereford, Holstein, Guernsey, or Polled Angus. By the early 1870s, dairymen manufactured more cheese than butter for the general trade. The Fox Valley had become well known as one of the finest dairy regions in the country. Elgin's central position in the Midwest dairy industry peaked in the 1890s. At this time, there were more than 200 cheese and butter factories within 60 miles of the city.

Around 1874, Dr. Joseph Tefft introduced his spectacular Friesian-Holstein cow, "Zwaan," which yielded 8 gallons of milk daily. Sylvester S. Mann's "Elgin Maid" was another famous producing cow. She was featured in the 1884 *Breeders' Gazette*.

B.W. Raymond, an outside investor in Elgin enterprises, and J.C. Adams were instrumental in the organization of the (Elgin) National Watch Company. The factory was offered to Elgin on the condition that 35 acres of land were donated and $25,000 in stock were subscribed by residents. Four men made sure that the conditions were met, and they were later dubbed the "immortals of Elgin." These men were Silvanus Wilcox, Walter L. Pease, Henry Sherman, and Benjamin F. Lawrence.

Machines used to make watch parts were built in the factory's machine department. Members of this department also kept the watch-making machines in good running order. There were ten divisions in the machine room: building, punch and die, fine tool, hardening and tempering, millwright, pattern, repair, tin shop, tool room, and blacksmith shop.

Here is the repair department all decked out for Christmas, as were practically all the departments during the holidays. During the mid-1920s, there were 75,500 machines used throughout the factory, and it was the duty of the repair department to see that all the machines in use were in good working order.

More products in greater quantities were produced in the screw department than any other department in the plant. There were 250 different sizes and kinds of screws and 550 separate winding bar and spring combinations catalogued. This group of men worked in the screw room in 1899.

THE PAGEANT OF TIME

By Krónos

BACKWARD, turn backward, O Time! Bring the Keepers of Minutes before us
—Passing in endless review, like a backwardspun film of the ages;
Guardians of Life's priceless hours, by their Maker entrusted to mortals—
All who have served thee most faithfully, back unto aeons forgotten!

Time waves a beckoning hand, with Life standing eager beside him.
Time turns the centuries back, like the hands of a watch in the winding.
Lo! What a myriad throng from the mists of the morning emerging—
See all the Keepers of Time, filing past in the march of the ages!

Far, far away in the land of the dinosaur, dragon and mammoth,
Back in that dim, distant dawn when creation steamed hot from the making,
See how the Cave-Man looks up from the rope over which he is musing,
Slow-burning marker of Time—in an age when Time groped for expression.

Babylon's ancient high priest, the wise and resourceful Berosus,
Points with the pride of a king to the shaft of the first brazen Sun-Dial.
Hark! In the Dance of the Hours, behold golden Greece in her glory,
Thrilled by the music and moonlight that flood the dim shrine of the Hour-Glass.

Borne high aloft by a slave, the ponderous gong of old Egypt
Throbs to the Water-Clock's warning that wing-footed daylight is passing.
Alfred the Great brings his Time-Candle, notched to betray how the minutes
(Counted by him in his wisdom as mortals' most priceless possession)

Ever and ever fled on. And near him the Barefooted Friar
Henlein, the fugitive craftsman whose Watch brought him pardon and honor.
Mark, too, the Nuremberg Egg, whose single hand, silently pointing,

Warned the Franconian lovers of gates grimly closing at midnight.
Boldly the swart buccaneer limps alongside his gleaming Sun-Cannon.
Hand in hand facing the future, Galileo and Marina Gamba
—With soft footfall, measured and slow, like the swing of the great lamp at Pisa—
March through the sorrows of life, linked by love even Time cannot alter.

Heedless of honor and fame, the squealing and struggling porker,
Shrilly lamenting the bristles that furnished Time's earliest Hair-springs,
Draws not so much as a glance from the dark eyes of Nicolas Facio,
Rapt, like the maid at his side, in the variant beauties of Jewels.

Elgin
MADE IN

"Father Time" was a logo featured in Elgin Watches advertisements. Before watches were mass produced, the ownership of a watch was regarded as a mark of prestige. Watches were assembled individually as hand work. Aaron L. Dennison experimented with watch-making machines and produced the first in 1850. N.B. Sherwood overhauled, improved, and added to the watch-making machinery. His designs for the interchangeable, precision parts were to become the standard of the industry. This was happening just as watches became more in demand due to the Civil War and the expansion of railroads. (JME.)

Lacking craftsmen on the frontier, the new Elgin National Watch Company founders hired a group of skillful craftsmen from all over New England to work in the Elgin factory. By the turn of the 20th century, Elgin was the leader of the watch industry. This 1922 ad shows the parade of "keepers of time." In the long line of time, the recent availability of watches is shown in the last two couplets. A little history lesson is given with this ad. (JME.)

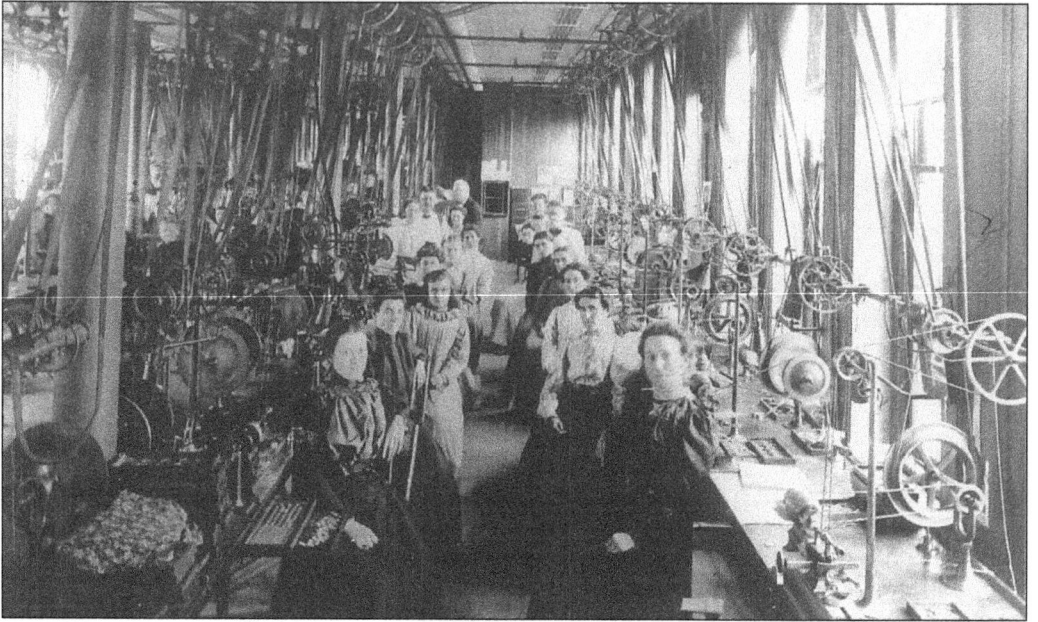

The gilding department thoroughly cleaned the parts sent from the plate and screw departments to remove grease, oil, and other foreign substances. Chemicals such as benzene, kayle, and cyanide, in addition to soap and water, were used in the cleaning processes. The parts were first electro-plated in nickel, then in silver, and dried in heated sawdust.

All of the pieces for a watch were placed in one of the compartments of a tray, like the one pictured here, and kept together through the gilding and assembling departments. Elgin watches were originally sold uncased to jewelers. The buyer selected a case from the local jeweler, and the jeweler "cased" the Elgin movement. (JME.)

1867

Elgin National Watch Company built a boardinghouse in the late 1860s to house craftsmen they brought to Elgin, because village accommodations were scarce. In the 1880s, the National House was built to replace the original boardinghouse. The four-story building had 150 rooms with steam heat and electric lights. This was the first of many employee benefits provided by the company.

The National House dining room could seat 500 people at one time. Hearty meals were included in the room rent, which cost a man $4.25 and cost a woman $3.35. The National House was in use for 66 years before it was torn down to make way for a parking lot.

These were employees of the dial room around 1890. Only the three standing women are identified. From left to right are as follows: Ada Kilbourne, Eva Evans, and Clara Tidmarsh. By the mid-1920s, there were an average of 5,800 finished dials turned out every working day. There were 363 different dial classifications of enamel or metal.

Elgin National Watch Company operated under the idea that a feeling of cooperation, of being needed, and of high regard, combined with cultural and physical benefits, made for increased productivity of the individual worker and greater success for the company. The company sponsored various sports teams and a gymnasium, picnics and get togethers, and bands and noon-time entertainment. These men from the motion room are relaxing at a stag party in 1896.

MOTION ROOM.
9-21-'12
Elgin WATCH WORKS.

Quare, an early clock maker, was the first to connect the watch hands to the watch train in such a way that the hour hand moved when the minute hand was set to time. Previously the two hands had to be set to time separately. When the hands are set to time together, the hour hand is turned at one-twelfth the speed of the minute hand by a wheel and pinion that turns on a stud fixed in the bottom plate.

The work of this young woman in the motion room of the Elgin National Watch Company was to put the plates, wheels, sleeves, and pinions, which carried the hour and minute hands, together—very delicate work! Notice that the workers are young women and that they have lamps to enhance the natural light that comes in from the windows.

OCTOBER 1906
Sun. Mon. Tues. Wed. Thurs. Fri. Sat.

NOVEMBER 1906
Sun. Mon. Tues. Wed. Thurs. Fri. Sat.

DECEMBER 19
Sun. Mon. Tues. Wed. Thurs. Fri.

FASHIONS OF THE 20th CENTURY.
and Elgin Watches, Standard of the Period. (actual size.)

ELGIN NATIONAL WATCH CO., Elgin, Ill.   FATHER TIME AND LADY ELGIN CALENDAR.

B.W. Raymond was a talented publicist, who kept the media up to date on developments in the nearly two years that it took to produce the first Elgin watch. When production was in full swing, the company had to warn the public about bogus "Elgin" watches that were being sold. The company was also pressured by foreign watchmakers and other American watchmakers. The making of watches from standard parts was news in those days, and Raymond took full advantage of this with articles in *Harpers New Monthly Magazine* and *Godey's Lady's Book*. Almanacs were distributed, and it was in these that "Father Time" was first used to identify Elgin watches. Calendars such as the one above were ever-popular, but up to a third of the advertising dollars were spent on magazine advertising. In the end, the name of Elgin came to be one of the top four most widely known of all trade names in America.

Three

RESCUE OF BODIES, BRAINS, AND SOULS

Reform movements were strong in America after the War of 1812. The country was bursting with enthusiasm and a belief in the ability to craft a "new world." Spurred on by this spirit of nationalism and faith in democracy and the common man was the willingness to experiment with social institutions and craft new approaches in the treatment of people who had previously not been provided for in a common way.

The people of the country wanted to create their own history, make their own native heroes, write their own kind of literature, and glory in their many different religions and churches. These religious institutions were among the first institutions in Elgin to use the arts to spread the word, with events such as the Chautauqua camps held in the early 1900s. Churches were gathering places for immigrants, with many holding services in the mother tongue.

Common, or public, schools and private schools were also instrumental in assimilating each new immigrant group. They dealt with the evil of nativistic feelings (fear of foreigners) from the children of previous immigrant groups.

The establishment in Elgin of the Illinois Northern Hospital for the Insane in 1869 offered an opportunity for forward-looking doctors to create more pleasant surroundings for those suffering from mental illness. While patients strolled at the hospital as part of their therapy, the saner residents of the city received their therapy for job fatigue by going out and having leisure-time fun. In the 1890s, that often meant playing a new popular sport, like rugby, which they called football. Elgin High boys competed with neighboring schools in this sport, back when it was merely a game and not an American institution.

This Elgin view is of the buildings on the west side of the river in 1866.

Founded in 1874 in Chautauqua, New York, the Chautauqua movement spread as the traveling assemblies took culture to small towns all over America. Elgin hosted assemblies from 1905 to 1910, and again from 1912 to 1914. Families camped in tents grouped around the main tent and dining hall and listened to music or speakers, such as William Jennings Bryan.

These early farmers were parishioners of St. John's Church in 1893. The girls in the front row are daughters of the Suchy and Kvidera families, and the boys are of the Kvidera and Rezek families. St. John's is now at Spring and Dexter Streets.

In 1862, the Reverend B. Thomas brought 100 newly liberated slaves to Elgin, and in 1866, the Second Baptist Church was organized for the former slaves, fostered by the Reverend A.J. Joslyn and others. The Fox River was used for baptisms even after the congregation had a home. This woman was one of five baptized on April 6, 1902.

This photograph shows one of the early Star Philathea classes with its teacher, W.A. Dickson. The Baraca-Philathea Union was founded around 1900, and the First Methodist Church of Elgin organized classes in 1908. The aim of the group was "to win a million for Christ." Their name meant "lovers of truth." Miss Henrietta Heron, of Elgin, promoted the establishment of the Baraca class for boys and the Star Philathea class for girls.

The Baptists formed the second church in Elgin, first meeting in Hezekiah Gifford's home, then later sharing the Elgin Chapel with the Congregational congregation. They bought the remaining interest in the Chapel in 1843, then built a cobblestone church in 1849, which they used until 1870, when they built a larger church that seated 1,200. Pictured here is part of the First Baptist Church choir, sometime between 1895 and 1902.

The Congregationalists were the first religious society in Elgin. James T. Gifford was the most prominent early member of the congregation. They shared the Elgin Chapel building until 1843. The Congregationalists built and used the basement of their new church, while the upper floors were still under construction. This architecturally interesting doorway is the main entrance to the church. (JME.)

The first Lutherans in the area were Germans, who worshiped at St. Johns beginning in October of 1859. The Swedish Lutherans formed Bethlehem Church, but Holy Trinity was the first English-speaking Lutheran church. Holy Trinity broke from Bethlehem in 1902 so that their children could worship "the faith of the fathers in the language of the children." These young people from Holy Trinity are having a Halloween party in 1910.

Elgin became incorporated in February 1854, and Dr. Joseph Tefft was the first mayor. This was the building used as Elgin's fourth city hall, which was first occupied in 1893. The tornado in 1920 damaged the building, weakening the structure, but it was not razed until 1969.

When the fourth city hall was built, Mayor William Grote donated the clock. You can see the face of this clock in the previous picture.

The Illinois Northern Hospital for the Insane was established by an act of the legislature in 1869. The City of Elgin purchased 150 acres of land along Route 31 on the southwest side of Elgin and donated it to the state for the hospital. The grounds around the buildings were artistically platted to produce the most calming and pleasing landscape effects, with miniature lakes, rustic bridges, and beautiful driveways and walks.

Patients began arriving in 1872. The buildings were designed to be as bright and sunlit as possible. Every effort was made to instill regular habits and to provide nourishing food, healthy employment, cheerful religious services, singing, reading, music, games, dancing, dramatic entertainment, and other pleasurable enjoyments for the patients.

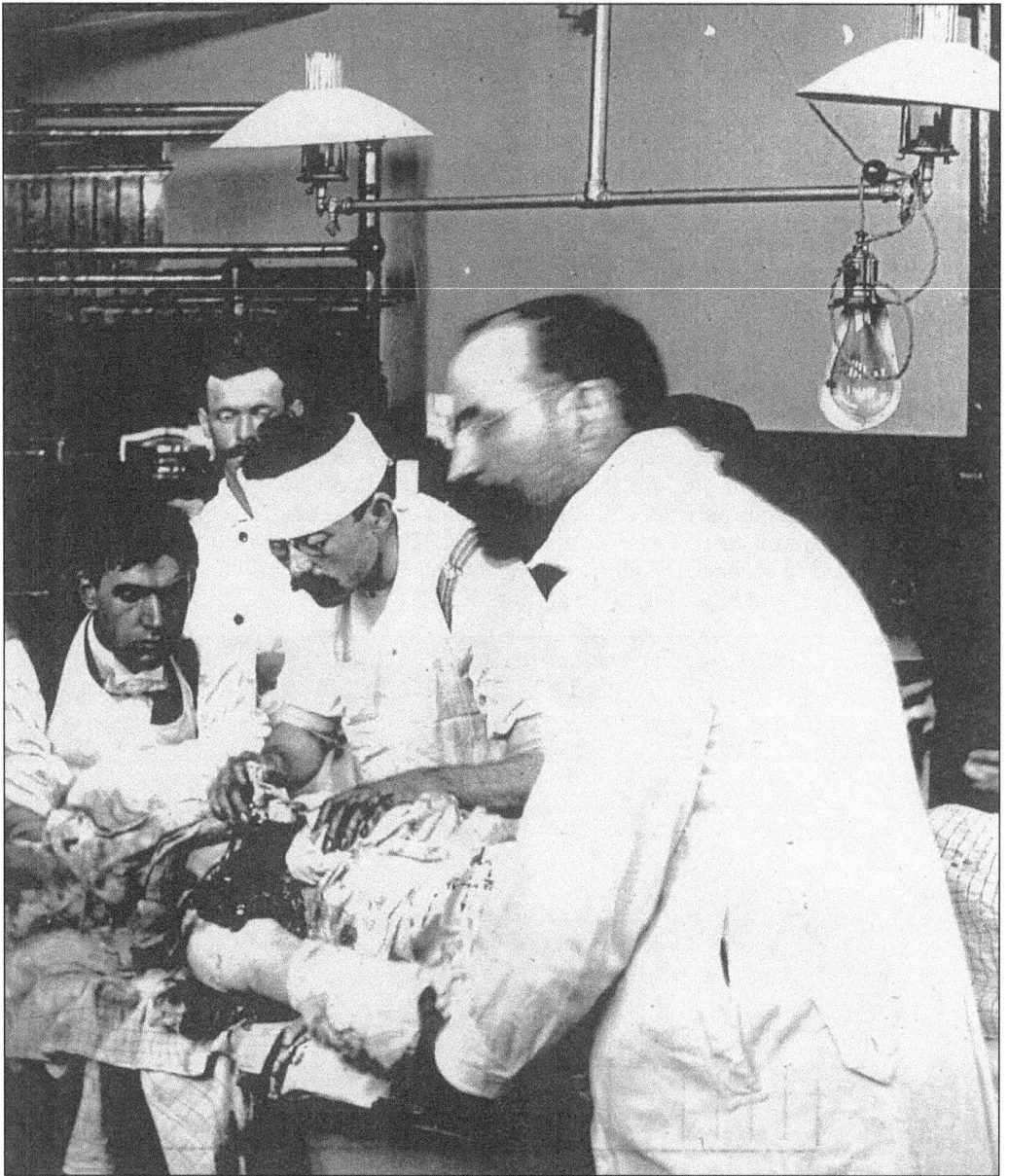

Sherman Hospital began as a gift of a two-story house on a large lot on Channing Street, from Henry Sherman to the Woman's Club. The club opened the hospital in July 1888 with six beds. During the first year of operation, 36 patients were admitted. Much of the food and the furnishings were donated by members of the Elgin Woman's Club. Shown here is an early candid photograph taken inside the operating room of the hospital.

Dr. Joseph Tefft was the first permanent physician in Elgin. Dr. C.A. Jaeger, above, was also an early physician. The 1857 city directory lists his office at Chicago Street, in the Commercial Block.

This is a portrait of Dr. Henry K. Whitford, who practiced in Elgin in the late 1800s. Dr. Whitford not only practiced in Elgin, but also taught at Bennett Medical College of Chicago. City directories list Henry K., Dan H., and Mrs. S.K. Whitford as Elgin physicians from 1884 to 1908.

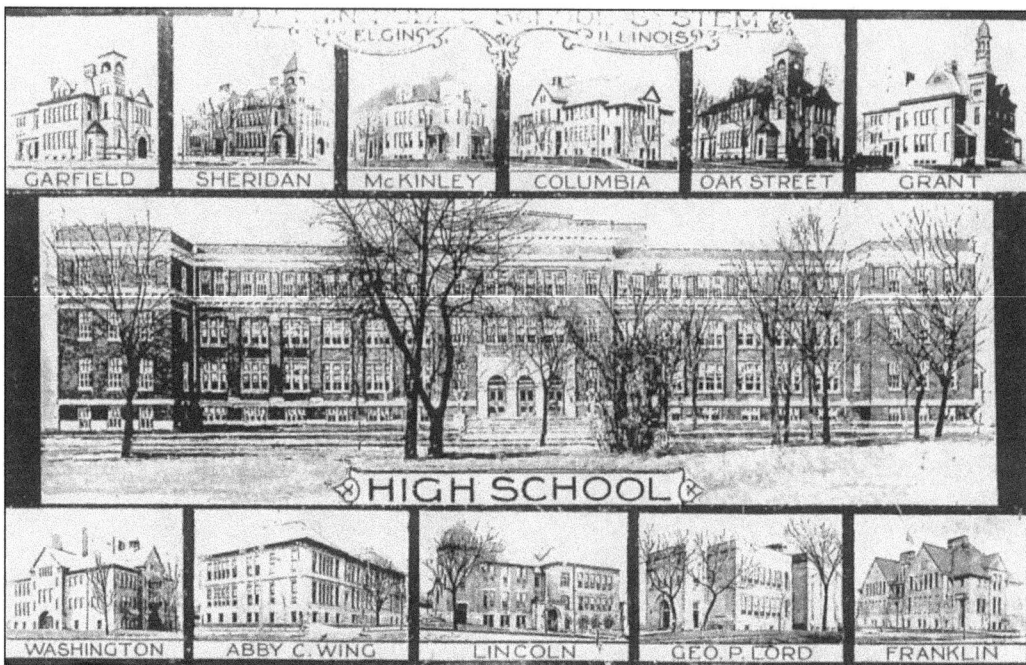

GARFIELD • SHERIDAN • McKINLEY • COLUMBIA • OAK STREET • GRANT

HIGH SCHOOL

WASHINGTON • ABBY C. WING • LINCOLN • GEO. P. LORD • FRANKLIN

The first school building was erected in 1837 and measured 24 feet by 30 feet. The Illinois Legislature mandated the first tax-supported, free school in 1851. By 1854, all Elgin schools were brought under the control of the city. By 1911, the above 11 schools were in use in Elgin.

Country schools were still is use in 1903. This one was in session seven months of the year, with an average daily attendance of six students. There were nine pupils enrolled, with a cost per-pupil-enrolled of $29.19 per year.

These Elgin High School teachers are standing in a biology lecture hall. Note the plant stem cross sections drawn on the blackboard and the science jars on the desk in this *c.* 1910 photograph. Students sat on bench seats for the lectures in this room.

These young women were part of a 1904 history class in the old Elgin High School. Pictured from left to right are Margaret Scheflow, Bessie Thomas Stroam, and Virginia Day Knodle.

This was the sixth-grade class of Columbia School in 1910. This school opened at Lincoln and Hill in 1893. Early students were taught that the study of the home neighborhood was the key to learning the geography of the world.

These 1923 McKinley School students seem to be engaged in a reading lesson. The early grades were taught from the blackboard, but older students used individual books. In addition to reading, pupils practiced listening to and memorizing hymns and poems and listening to the reading or telling of fairy tales, myths, and stories. McKinley is located at Prospect and Lovell Streets.

This second Elgin High School building was completed in 1884 and used until 1910, when it was razed. This was the first school in which each pupil had a desk of his own. The picture was taken from Gifford Park, sometime between 1893 and 1895.

This is the three-time state high school champion Elgin High School football team of 1896. Football was much more informal in those days. Uniforms were not standardized, and games were not on a set schedule. The ball was also a rounder ball than the one used today. The boys from Elgin High played against the boys from Elgin Academy annually.

Elgin Seminary was founded in the spring of 1851 by the Misses Emily and Ellen E. Lord for the education of young ladies. There were times, however, when young men were also admitted. The school continued until the summer of 1856.

Judge and Mrs. Nathaniel Sears left a bequest to Elgin Academy that paid the bills during the Depression. Another of their gifts was the Laura Davidson Sears Academy of Fine Arts, completed in 1924, and a collection of art including a full-length portrait of George Washington by Gilbert Stuart to be displayed in the building.

Four

RAILS, CARS, AND FACTORIES

Elgin's growth was stunted for a brief time between 1857 and the Civil War. But by the 1870s, the city's economy was off and running. This post-war boom period would have been impossible without substantial capital to feed the fires of business. Elgin's many financial institutions of the day did not allow the entrepreneurs of industry to run out of money. This decade saw the establishment in Elgin of a plow factory, Vollor & Company's chewing gum factory, and the Wilder & Josyln Brickworks, which was producing 5 million bricks a year by 1875! The Elgin Packing Company was producing 300,000 cans of fruits and vegetables a year for American homes across the country.

Elgin products not only found their way into all areas of the U.S., but also into the international market with watches, canned goods, and Bibles being exported. Historians R. Waite Joslyn and Frank W. Joslyn noted in a 1908 work that even people in China knew of the city of Elgin. "The missionary in far-off China reads to his almond-eyed pupils out of a Bible made at D.C. Cook's publishing house, accompanies their hymns on an organ from the Seybold factory, closes school by looking at an Elgin watch, and then goes to his home to make tea out of water drawn by an Elgin windmill, and sweetens it with condensed milk prepared at the Brook street factory." The one single product that especially put Elgin on the map and still serves to identify the town is the Elgin watch.

Getting anywhere was generally not a problem for the citizens of Elgin. An excellent transportation system linked the city to the whole country. Electric trolleys, third-rail trains, the Chicago & Northwestern railroad, and automobiles soon replaced horses and buggies as the preferred personal means of travel.

This 1866 view of Elgin was photographed by John M. Adams. In his time, Elgin still maintained its rural character with fenced meadows, fields, and trees. This panoramic look at Elgin has a Currier-and-Ives feeling to it. Note the single power line suspended by poles along the west bank.

If a town wanted to survive and grow in the late 1800s, the railroad had to play a part, for without a railroad to quickly deliver agricultural products to market, the slower horse and wagon limited the life of these products. Railroading also included city-based, horse-drawn car lines, overhead electric trolley lines, and, eventually, third-rail interurban lines. This early photograph shows workmen laying track on a residential street.

Prior to 1890, the modern way to get around town was by rail car drawn by horses. This view of Douglas Street looking south shows the rail going straight down the center of the street, with room on either side of the rails to accommodate horse-drawn buggies and wagons. Telephone and light poles ribbon each side of the street.

Conductors of the Elgin electric street cars pause outside the car barn in this almost 100-year-old photograph. The cars were powered by overhead electrical lines. This building had three tracks leading out to the left and a single track exiting to the right. The car in the barn is the one that serviced Grove Avenue.

Both of these photographs were made by Christie. For its day, this was quite an action shot, in that it recorded passengers leaving the Elgin 204 car on the left. Passengers wait to board an Aurora 106 car to the right, on a rainy day in July 1908. Notice the complicated gridwork of electrical lines running out of the barn.

At one time in the early part of the 20th century, one could travel all the way from Elgin to New York by trains using electricity and going at a decent rate of speed. Arthur Eck shot this view, *c.* 1907, of motorman Claude Campbell and conductor George Reber outside their car. Fares for travel were cheap at that time.

STREET SCENE

If you think that navigating in a big city is a hassle today, take a look at what it was like in 1902 in downtown Elgin. The electric cars have the streets jammed, and the conductor was having to constantly re-attach the pole, which rested on the overhead electric line, when they negotiated sharp corners.

Auto production was booming by 1907, with hundreds of garages producing their own version of an idea that was too simple and basic to patent. VanWambeke & Sons manufactured their own version of the auto, called the Van Motor Wagon, in a workshop located on Jefferson Street. Each of these cars has different coach works. Only eight of these cars were built between 1907 and 1909.

Here is a familiar scene to commuters of today. The livery stables have sent their "cabbies" out to meet the train. Two young train spotters are sitting on the side of a cart waiting for the train to appear. This moment in time was recorded at the Chicago, Milwaukee & St. Paul railroad station in Elgin.

Benjamin Lawrence and Walter L. Pease shut down their distillery plant, pooled their assets with M.C. Town, and started up a new bank in June of 1865. Here we see various checks used by this new bank, the First National Bank of Elgin, with one dating back to the 1870s, and a deposit slip from 1908 listing a series of checks made out for 3¢, 2¢, and 12¢!

The most famous president of the First National Bank was George P. Lord, who was also the business manager of the watch company, owner of a dairy farm, mayor of the city, and, at one time, president of the Elgin Board of Education. He gave his support to parks, the hospital, the YMCA, and Elgin Academy. Here we have the well-lit interior of a bank in the pre–World War I period.

54

Demarcus Clark operated an early bank out of his store in the 1850s, and in 1855, Orlando Davidson, son-in-law of city founder James T. Gifford, started his own bank. Many of these early banks proved to be short-lived due to bad investments. Such was the case of Davidson's banks, which had purchased Confederate States of America bonds. Banks of this time issued their own colorful paper money. These notes are from Clark's Elgin Bank.

Thomas McBride was born in Ireland and brought to the U.S. and Elgin by his parents in the 1860s. His father, Henry, established a modest coal and wood business in town, and when Thomas left school, he joined his father in business. Soon their business included the selling of coke, lime, and cement.

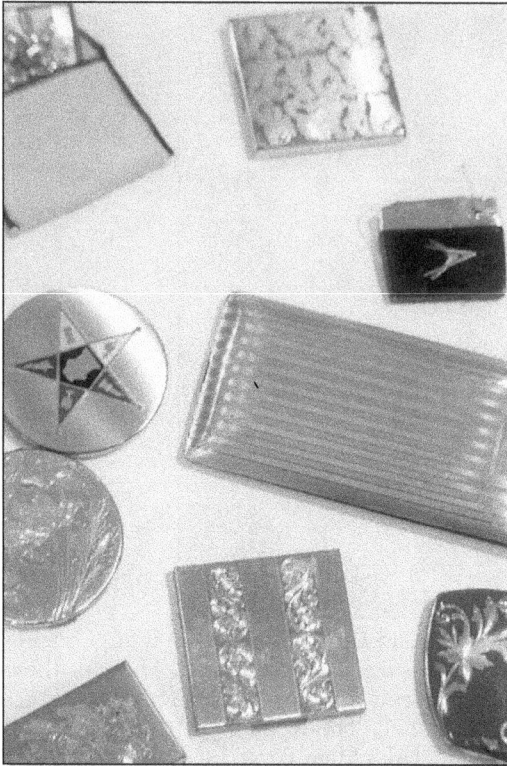

The Illinois Watch Case Company began to diversify and produce compacts for the new cosmetics industry in the 1920s and 1930s. Movies and Max Factor were responsible for creating a desire in women to look as good as the movie stars. As more and more women were introduced to pre-rolled cigarettes, women's lighters came into vogue in the 1930s. (JME.)

In his film *Modern Times*, Charlie Chaplin poked fun at the fast-paced, machine-driven factory work and showed workers as the slaves of the huge machinery. This view of *Ben at the Press Cast Factory*, taken in the Elgin National Watch Company factory, makes the same point. Ben was photographed by Dr. Peter Campbell around 1900, at a time when power came down from long revolving shafts, by way of rubber and leather belting, to the crowded machines on the floor.

This young, all-male work crew, many of whom are of German heritage, is hard at work making bread. The men worked for the Kind Baking Company, which was found on McBride Street. Note the fancy tin roof. From left to right, the workers are as follows: Frank ?, Joseph Kastner, Joe Thums, Ernest (Erni) Benz, John Dietz, and William Schmit.

This postcard view of the factory shows that it was almost three stories. This new building dates from 1910. The chimney of the bakery is seen to the left, and railroad tracks run along the side of the building. A bread wagon is set to take off on a delivery.

David C. Cook learned his father's trade—the craft of printing. He was evangelical in faith, and in 1872, he organized a Sunday school in Chicago named Everybody's Mission. Finding few printed materials available for his class, he published a teacher's magazine in 1875. By May of 1882, his business had outgrown its location, so he moved to a new factory in Elgin. By 1883, the presses were busy 24 hours a day with a work force of over 300.

By 1908, the David C. Cook plant had 12 associate editors, who were connected to various evangelical churches in the area, and hundreds of writers as part of the production team working on Sunday school materials. Cook treated his workers fairly. In 1900, he cut the hours from ten to nine each day, and in 1911, he reduced them to eight.

Labor strikes and walkouts plagued the Selz Shoe factory in 1898 and 1899. The previous owners had sold out to the Selz-Schwab & Co. of Chicago in 1897 due to actions by the newly formed Elgin Trades Council, an umbrella for the machinist, baker, cigar makers, and shoe worker unions. The tornado of 1920 destroyed the roof and second floor, and the crash forced the factory to close.

Before the days of pasteurization, every community brewed its own beer. It was brewed and consumed daily, for it could not be transported long distances. It was delivered to the local bars, where one could take a standard-sized, shallow pail with a lid, called a growler, to be filled for home consumption. The early 1854 Eagle Brewery was owned by C. Althen. The new plant shown here was much larger and produced "Adler Brau."

In 1908, reporter A.H. Kirkland of the *Elgin Daily Courier* reported that the Seybold Piano and Organ Company was one of Elgin's "strongest bidders for foreign trade . . . the company has shipped organs to England, Scotland, Norway, Denmark, Germany, Holland, Australia, Columbia, Mexico, Cuba, and Canada." This is the action department where keyboards were made. (JME.)

In the years prior to World War I, production shifted away from organ building to the piano, especially the manufacture of player pianos. An ill-fated merger with another manufacturer ended in bankruptcy, but Emil P. Johnson of Ottawa took over the abandoned building. One of the most desirable player pianos to ever roll out of the factory was the P.C. Weaver, Elgin-made by the Seybold Piano Company. (JME.)

Cyrus Woodruff first started out in Elgin in 1879 with an iron works on Lake Street. His 25 workers made castings for school and opera seating and later, with the addition of a partner, made various castings for the farm trade. Eighty thousand opera chairs were manufactured in 1887, along with thousands of school desks, all with only 50 workers. Cyrus was joined in the business by his son, Charles, in the 1880s. It then became a leading manufacturer of coffee and flour grinding mills for grocers. The company's line of 40 grinders ranged from table-top models to large, colorful, red or maroon floor-mounted units. The largest coffee grinders could process 7 pounds of coffee with one loading.

This view of employees in the foundry shows the workers preparing to take large coffee grinder wheels out of the molds. Work in a foundry was one of the hottest and most backbreaking jobs one could find. Most workers found better jobs and moved on. For this reason, immigrants were hired, and they were hired at a very low wage. Many ethnic groups came to Elgin and worked in the foundry. Hungarians were followed by Hispanics in the 1920s, and black workers came from the South in the 1950s. During World War II, a group of Puerto Ricans were recruited to help produce propeller, wench, and motor castings for the military.

Five

THE GREAT WAR: AT HOME AND OVER THERE

In the late summer of 1914, the dogs of war ran wild when the world powers turned their weapons on each other. By August, the "Great War" was on, and the United States, as in so many other wars, was fearful of becoming involved. President Wilson asked people to remain neutral but probably knew that if the war was a long one, this country could not escape an economic and military role.

Elgin was uneasy about the war in Europe because much of its population was made up of people from opposite sides. The city's German population, prior to United States involvement in the war, sided with their mother country, raising money for the German Red Cross. They pressured for the United States to strictly adhere to the policy of neutrality.

Once the United States declared war in April 1917, it became evident that in order to win this long, drawn-out war, we would not only have to make loans and send supplies, but also send soldiers to break the stalemate.

Elgin, in a patriotic fervor, sent their doughboys off with massive parades, dinners, and speeches and welcomed them back in a like manner. At home, they also did their part as civilian soldiers of democracy.

Elgin's Company E of the 3rd Regiment marches off to war on September 13, 1918, across the Chicago Street Bridge. They boarded a train at the west side Northwestern station, which would take them to Camp Logan, Texas, for training.

August was the month in 1918 that Selective Service Boards in the United States started drafting 18 to 45-year-old men, and by the end of the war, over 24 million Americans had been registered for the draft. Of that number, 2.8 million were drafted into the army, and close to 2 million were shipped off to France, but less than that figure saw active service. Elgin had a multitude of young men ready and willing to help the Allies in the war. This non-uniformed group of young recruits seems anxious to get to France and get it all over with quickly. The distinguished-looking gentleman to the right in the front row seem to be officials of some kind, perhaps from the Selective Service Board. Posters played a big part in encouraging men to volunteer for war. The famous Joseph Leyendecker "Weapons for Liberty" poster, produced in 1918 to encourage Boy Scouts to sell bonds in the Third Liberty Loan, is in the window of the store behind the men.

September 13, 1918, was a special day for Elgin and surrounding communities. This was the day that Elgin's Company E left town and headed for training in Texas, before shipping off to join our new Allies in France. Flags were everywhere, and cars and people packed the area around the railroad station. People crowded as close as they could to the tracks to get one last look at a loved one.

Somewhere in the crowd that day there must have been a military band like the Loyal Order of Moose Drum and Bugle Corp, shown here on top of a passenger car, which played for Elgin's first draft group in 1917. American soldiers of this war were lucky to be hailed as heroes leaving the country and as heroes on their return.

The passenger cars were filled with Elgin's uniformed soldiers who had answered the wake-up call from Europe asking for more men to fight the forces of evil. Suddenly Europe's war had become our war, and many young men could not wait to be sent into action and show the Kaiser a thing or two. Soldiers in this photograph reach out of the car windows to touch a loved one once more.

Corporal Alvin Henry Wilkening was a member of Company E. This photograph of Wilkening beside his horse is as romantic an image of World War I as could be found. He was in Larochette, Luxemburg, and wrote, "Aren't I a tough looking bird? Well, rather." The overseas pictures in this chapter are taken from his album.

When Wilkening and his unit made it to the front in France, they witnessed a landscape like another planet—a dead zone. The trenches spread all across France and were littered with bodily remains and mangled war machines. This is all captured in this photograph titled "Bethincourt in the Somme Valley."

Trenches were built by both sides under the cover of darkness, and spread from the North Sea to Switzerland, a distance of 600 miles. They were usually 5-feet deep and 2-feet wide and were sometimes hundreds of yards apart and other times so close that you could talk to the enemy. Beneath major fortifications, such as these "swan trenches," one can see the dugouts used by soldiers to survive shelling by the enemy.

Sanitation was a real problem. Corpses of men and horses and their excrement covered the land, polluting rivers, streams, and wells. This photographer captures his mates bringing up water from a well, which has signs warning of pollution. In the background, there is what he noted was a "swell bivy (bivouac)." Standing shelters were a treat for the advancing Americans, who usually stayed in canvas tents or dugouts.

Elgin's Company E became part of the 129th Infantry, 33rd (Prairie) Division, and arrived in time to participate in the Meuse-Argonne offensive. In the "Record of Events and Roster of the 129th U.S. Infantry," one soldier rhymed, "The forest where once was primeval and grand, is marked by the plots where the blasted pines stand. Its groves, once untrampled where Yank blood was shed are watched every night by the sentinel dead."

The Germans who survived the Allied bombardment used pill boxes to wreak havoc on the advancing enemy. Machine guns sprayed the horizon through narrow, horizontal slits. L.J. Sandberg, an Elgin soldier, described one attempt to dislodge the Germans when, in one three-hour period, 80,000 shells were fired. He noted, "it kind of makes a fellow feel like ducking his head and stay [sic] close to the ground."

While good Elgin doughboys were encouraged by their training to kill Germans, back home, German-hating in a town inhabited by a sizable German-American population seemed inevitable. Tempers heated to the boiling point. Elginites took to the streets to show what they would do to Kaiser Wilhelm II if they had a chance. Note "Uncle Sam" on top of the hearse.

HUNTING THE HUN

WORDS BY
HOWARD E. ROGERS

MUSIC BY
"ARCHIE GOTTLER

Back on the Elgin home front, peoples' lives were as controlled as that of the doughboy's. They were taught that everything German was bad, even music by long-ago, dead German composers. A typical anti-German song that may have been sung in Elgin parlors was "Hunting the Hun." Its lyrics stated, "First you get a gun. Then you look for a Hun." (JME.)

Piano rolls featured the latest tin pan alley's attempt to cash in on the war. Tunes were written to say that the "home fires were burning" for the soldiers over there and that their sweethearts would be waiting for their return while getting the work at home done. (JME.)

70

George Creel, as head of the newly created Committee on Public Information, kept people at home doing their part to win the war, while soldiers were fighting in Europe. Everyone had a role to play, young and old alike. Children were encouraged to buy savings stamps, and adults were regarded as suspicious unless they bought war bonds. Elgin factories supplied uniform shirts, lathes, and watches for the war. (JME.)

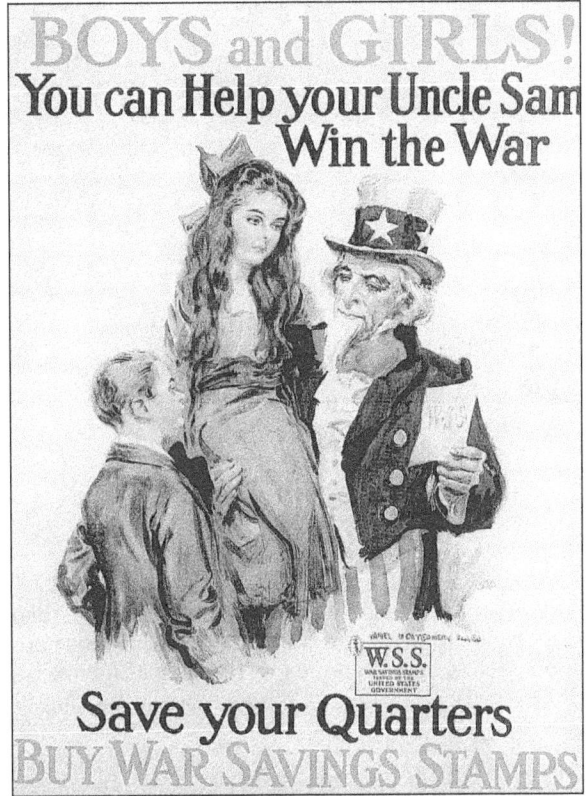

BOYS and GIRLS!
You can Help your Uncle Sam
Win the War

W.S.S.
WAR SAVINGS STAMPS
ISSUED BY THE
UNITED STATES
GOVERNMENT

Save your Quarters
BUY WAR SAVINGS STAMPS

Elgin's youth also did their part. This photograph, taken in the rear of Mable Adams's home at 428 Division Street, shows a group of boys playing at war. Mable's father, one of Elgin's important photographers, had this photograph made into a postcard for sale to patriotic citizens.

Americans were encouraged to plant victory gardens. The Elgin High School students made real contributions to the war in 1918 and 1919 when they "did without sweaters, abolished caps and gowns, secured money for the soldier's memorial, adopted a French orphan, bought $1,500 in Liberty Bonds, sent 2,000 books to soldiers, and furnished 10 men for service." (JME.)

Tanks were never battle winners, but they did scare the enemy, encourage morale, and act as shields from enemy fire. The British tank had a nine-man crew. The tank shown here is a "male' tank, in that it had a six pounder gun on each side and one machine gun. The "female" tanks had two machine guns instead. The Brits had 49 such tanks in the Battle of the Somme, but 17 broke down on the way to the front.

Munitions manufacturer Krupp supplied the Germans with extraordinary guns and shells. Projectiles such as these "big boys from Jerry (Germans)" reigned terror on the Allies. These could be fired from 20 miles away. "Big Bertha," named for Gustav Krupp's wife, could fire all the way across the English Channel.

The French wanted to use American men as replacements, fighting under the flag of France. The Americans pressured to fight in all-American groups. Eventually they did, but many soldiers fought bravely in integrated units. This colorful parade of soldiers, photographed in Metz in December 1918, shows the American element in this army flying the Star Spangled Banner and infantry flags behind the French tricolor.

At the end of the war, the 129th served as part of the occupation army in Luxembourg. Thirty-eight Elgin soldiers did not return. Most died in battle, but some died of disease. Soldiers brought back memories of battles, deaths, and bravery but left behind a devastated Europe. Land had to be reclaimed for farming, towns had to be reconstructed, and churches, such as this shelled Albert Cathedral, had to be brought back to life.

Pandemonium ruled in Elgin on November 11, 1918, as young and old deserted their work, schools, and homes to run into the street to celebrate the end of the war. By the time the soldiers arrived home on June 14, 1919, the town had planned a splendid Welcome Day Parade, as well as many special events. The townspeople built a Victory Arch and secured a huge flag, to be held by what appears in this photograph to be costumed American Indians.

Insignias of Elgin's fighting men's military units were placed on the arches, as was the "Welcome." Crowds lined the Chicago Street bridge, and every light pole was flying an American flag in tribute. It must have been a sunny day by the time the fighting units passed in review, because many of the ladies are holding umbrellas.

Center Street was blocked off, and six long banquet tables were placed in the center for a special welcome-home meal for the returning heroes. Sixty women in white are busy working on the table settings for a "meal the boys would never forget." Plenty of good, safe Elgin milk was on hand, with over a dozen huge milk cans stacked on the corner.

It appears that Elgin's prettiest young ladies were selected to serve the returning soldiers. The plates are loaded with fresh bananas and apples, and a metal milk pitcher is resting on a chair. Some of the soldiers' faces seem to show strained pleasure. It was hard to make the leap from "over there" to "over here"—from the nightmare of war back to their young lives at home.

Every American town wanted to memorialize their fighting soldiers after the end of the war, and Elgin's bronze doughboy at Prairie and Villa is a realistic representation of that sentiment. With its aged patina of green and black, it captures the rugged, grimy nature of war. The face is resolute and brave, with idealistic eyes. (JME.)

Six

CULTURE COMES TO TOWN

Much of Elgin's love of the arts came to town with the arrival of the Germans. In the mid-1800s, much of Europe was in political and ethnic turmoil. In 1871, the State of Germany was formed out of various German-speaking kingdoms, minus Austria. Germans who were of the Jewish faith found it additionally advantageous to escape to the New World from yet another pogrom or ethnic cleansing. Many of the German immigrants who settled in Elgin were Jewish. It was during the late 19th century that major American cities such as Chicago began to establish symphonies. Concert halls across the land were filled by German musicians playing the music of German composers.

The many churches and a lively list of newspapers also contributed to a cultural climate. Schools played their part by presenting music and art instruction from the early grades through high school. Various vaudeville acts played the local opera houses, and the Watch Factory Band became the musical backbone of the city.

Cultural societies were all the rage in Elgin. In 1887, the Elgin Woman's Club, which encouraged art, literature, music, and science, was meeting twice a month at the YWCA, and by 1908, the city had several musical and literary societies.

This is downtown Elgin in 1882, showing the east side of the river and, in the foreground, the west-side railroad tracks.

Harry Eduard Miller, son of William C. and Bertha, was born in 1878. He became a first-class violinist, who was first-chair violinist with the Russian Symphony Orchestra of New York. He was also part of Victor Herbert's orchestra and the New York Philharmonic. Later in his career, he taught at a Chicago conservatory and played in Hollywood movie orchestras.

Joseph Hecker, Elgin's most famous musician, was hired by the Elgin National Watch Factory in 1886 to build its band to a musical level high enough that it could tour the country as an advertisement for the company's watches. He also served as the conductor of the youthful Slayton Women's Symphony Orchestra. His three musical daughters played in this orchestra.

THE SLAYTON WOMAN'S SYMPHONY ORCHESTRA
JOSEPH HECKER, Conductor

In 1870, Elgin's first DuBois Opera House was built using Fox River Valley white brick, with two stores on the first floor and the opera house, which seated 1,500, on the second. It was a hall where traveling acts, as well as local bands, could perform. The spectacular Chicago Marine Band appeared at the DuBois Opera House in 1895.

DuBois Opera House....

ELGIN, ILLINOIS,

Friday, September 27th, 1895.

T. P. BROOKE, Conductor.

THE CHICAGO MARINE BAND

Greatest Popular Music Band in America.

HOWARD PEW, Manager.

200 Wabash Avenue. ....CHICAGO.

The Chicago Marine Band was under the direction of T.P. Brooks at the time of this ad. He made sure that his players were colorfully dressed and performed the latest hit music. In an era of ragtime music and the popular two step, Brooks started writing his own musical compositions in these two new musical genres for performances mixed with more traditional band music.

SONG OF THE ELGIN WATCH.

Composed for ELGIN ALMANAC, 1874.

Words and Music by P. P. BLISS.

1. "Here am I," said the watch, "With a nim-ble spring To my life work now I go,
2. "Shall I smile in the face Of a la-dy fair? To her neck with a chain be bound?
3. "Shall I tell of the hour When a death-less soul To this mor-tal life has come?
4. "Here am I, at my post, And in an-y case In my own or a dis-tant clime,

On-ly give me the key And a song I'll sing, Keeping time nei-ther fast nor slow."
Shall I hang by a cord To a shop wall bare? Or go sail-ing the world a-round?"
Shall my heart beat the time While the bell doth toll For the child in the an-gels' home?"
Let my life tell to all, Who behold my face, Of the worth of the jew-el, time."

CHORUS.

"Wherev-er I may be, On the land or on the sea, This one thing well I'll do, I'll do

Go on and on, Like the roll-ing sun, And ev-er, ev-er-more be true

The art of advertising blossomed in the industrial age that followed the Civil War. Factories had to make sure their products were chosen over similar products. The young Elgin National Watch Company published an almanac that included information about the factory. Included in the first almanac in 1874 was the "Song of the Elgin Watch." Half a million copies of this almanac were distributed nationwide.

Hecker's Band spread the word about Elgin watches from coast to coast. The band played at the Ice Palace in St. Paul, the St. Louis Fair of 1887, and two national Republican conventions (1888 and 1892). Hecker imported players from all over the U.S. to work in the factory and play in his band.

The Elgin Opera House,
February 6th and 7th, 1896.

Minstrel Performance by the.....

Grand Ethiopean Nightingales.

For the benefit of Sherman Hospital and Local Charities. . . . .
. . . . . 40 Performers, Costumed by Worthless, of Paris, Ill.

Manager and Musical Director - Miss Stella Hale
Director of Orchestra   -   Mr. J. F. Tetzner

PATRONESSES

Mrs. Wilson H. Doe,
Mrs. Wm. F. Hunter,
Mrs. J. M. Blackburn,
Mrs. John S. Wilcox,
Mrs. C. L. Chamberlain,
Mrs. R. D. Holembeak.

PRINTED AND DESIGNED BY....
C. T. VAN GORDER,
HOME BANK BLOCK. - ELGIN, ILL.

The minstrel show was a popular form of entertainment at the turn of the 20th century. These shows started out as all-black touring companies that reveled in their ethnicity by poking fun in a way that white audiences found humorous. In 1896, the Grand Ethiopean [sic] Nightingales appeared at the Elgin Opera House.

Victorian America was not all that prim and proper in private, and young people of Elgin began to set the pace for a looser society that would emerge in the early 20th century. Children of all ages liked to dress up and play other people, even those of the opposite sex. This group had a grand time exchanging roles. This photograph is also an excellent study of how a middle-class parlor was decorated in the late 1800s.

Elgin audiences must have talked about this stage show for days. This striking theatrical cast photograph was taken by an Elgin photographer in the early 1930s. This play must have had a rather bizarre story line, for there is a comical cowboy, two or three female impersonators, three

Chinese people, and a man in black face. In the back rows are over a dozen "coolies," many of which are carrying Chinese lanterns. On the fringe of the theatrical group, to the right, are the managers of the production.

This photograph of the DuBois Opera House offers a rare view of the manner in which the hall and stage were constructed. Ordinary wooden chairs were numbered so that ticket holders could find their seat. The ceiling is vaulted and colorfully stenciled. The stage is decorated with Corinthian columns, with a rope trim over the stage. Various backdrops can be seen behind the musicians sitting on stage.

Joseph Hecker was born in Austria. While living in England, he met Jane Astin, and they were married. Four musical children were born to the Heckers. The children appeared in concert at the DuBois Opera House with their father and the Elgin Military Band in 1889. Pictured above, from left to right, are as follows: Carl, Berta, Cecile, and Stella. Joseph Hecker died in 1917.

With Longfellow's poem for inspiration, Mina Lee Brady, a dramatics teacher, produced Elgin's first Hiawatha Pageant. Carl Parlasca was the true father of the festival, however, which began in the 1920s. He was a Boy Scout leader whose knowledge of American Indian lore kept his young campers mesmerized. Parlasca viewed the festival as a way to tell about the variety and greatness of the American Indians and their civilizations. Pictured here are two early pageant actors.

Parlasca was a stickler for details when it came to the complicated American Indian dances taught to him by Eddie Little Chief, a member of the Rosebud Sioux. By the 1950s, these colorful pageants were drawing audiences of nearly 10,000. Parlasca was adopted as a brother by tribes of Sioux, Blackfeet, and Ojibway.

Wives and daughters of wealthy and middle-class husbands began to dabble in paints by the 1870s. Miss S.H. Lang had a studio in West Elgin, where men and women could receive instruction. This well-composed photograph, c. 1890s, shows Miss Lang in a rocker taking her eyes off her pupils long enough to give the cameraman a most stern look.

These young ladies in period dress could be set to perform at the opera house or merely posed in a photographer's studio. The three girls in front are holding fans, which add to the dramatic moment. Girls of this period all wore their hair parted in the middle and flowing, or else drawn up in a bun or two. The personality of each of the girls shines through in this excellent image of a day gone forever.

In the 1930s, Elgin had a hard-working sculptor named Trygve Rovelstad, with the flare and style of Lorado Taft. He wanted to cast a four-figure, 12-foot-tall group for the centennial of Elgin in 1935. A foundation was completed in Davidson Park, and models of the four-member pioneer family were completed, but the project failed for lack of funds. A head representing the Gifford brothers that he sculpted is in the square in front of Hemmens Auditorium. (JME.)

Lester Sackett had a studio at 17 Douglas. He was the first photographer on the scene to record the Johnstown flood. He was not only a professional photographer, but also a sculptor, a lecturer, and a Bethel Commander of the Knights Templer in Elgin. His wife, Mary, was a fourth grade teacher in the Elgin school system. This image of Sackett is from the early 1900s.

Elgin was home to Albert W. Kenney, a landscape painter in the 1880s. He had a studio at 47 East Chicago Street. If his artistic talent was on a par with the skills of the photographer, then he was a fine artist indeed. Kenney, along with the tools of his trade—canvas, tripod, and paint pallet—stares directly at the camera lens to complete the realism of the photograph and make it a true work of art. Early camera film was very slow and needed long exposure time. The longer the subject of a studio portrait had to stand still, the greater risk of a blurred image. Because of this problem, concealed metal head braces were sometimes used.

Gerlach was a later Elgin photographer who had a studio at the corner of Douglas and Division. At the turn of the 20th century, photographers delivered the pictures glued to stiff boarding sized 4 1/4-x-6 1/2 inches to keep them from curling. Many cards also had a thin tissue sheet that folded over the image to protect its shiny finish. This tissue, featuring two spiders and a web, is most unusual. You can see a young man through the tissue. (JME.)

John Manly Adams photographed his studio in 1866. This is a masterful raised-elevation shot. The photograph was taken with a very fast lens, because the horses are dead-on focused with only slight head motion. One can easily see the hanging pocket watches in the jewelry shop window and make out all the photographs mounted on the wall of Adams's studio.

On the surface, this *c.* 1901 photograph of Elgin's Dr. Roy P. Wilson with his wife and child does not appear to be out of the ordinary. But, if you look closely, you can see that the good doctor has triggered the shot himself using a long cord, shown here running in front of his left pants leg. A clever shot—even the horse agrees with a gentle nod of his head!

There is an artistic streak running through us all, a desire to do something a little different. This unknown Elgin photographer has turned an ordinary shot of two fellows into a work of art by exposing one side of the negative, then having the men shift to the other side of the tree for their second "shot." The two exposures are almost perfectly balanced.

90

Seven

PARADES, RACES, AND BUSTER BROWN

From the end of the 19th century through the Great War, the United States was riding an emotional patriotic high. During these years, our country became an imperialistic power, creating a country and building "our" Panama Canal to connect two oceans. Elgin did not have to be convinced to celebrate, and it showed the flag on all public occasions.

In this period, traveling circuses and carnival shows became bigger and better, just as our nation boasted of being bigger and better. One-ring circuses gave way to two and then three rings. The simple parades through the streets became spectacles in themselves, complete with the circus band and decorated wagons filled with exotic animals. Circuses joined in when groups such as the Elks staged parades, and the streets were packed with entertainment-seeking Elginites. Fun and leisure-time activities had become big business in America.

The automobile race came into its own before World War I, and Elgin had one of the earliest and best annual automobile races in the country until the 1920s. The city even had a fictional character, Buster Brown, "come to life and live in Elgin." Buster Brown was the creation of the legendary cartoonist Richard Outcault and dates from 1902. His faithful companion was a mean-looking, talking bulldog by the name of Tige. The cartoon strip did not last long after World War I, but the dog and boy became associated with many products, such as the show company that picked the dynamic duo as their symbol at the World's Fair in 1904. In August of 1918, a three-year-old child was picked up in Chicago while wandering the streets. He was dressed in a white Buster Brown outfit, and when the press got wind of the story, he was dubbed Buster Brown. He was not parentless, but he was adopted by an Elgin attorney, William A. Paulson, and his wife and brought to live for a time at 303 River Bluff Road. Buster did not live happily ever after, however, for through a series of misfortunes, he winds up completing his youth with another set of parents on a small farm in Indiana.

This is the shoreline of the Fox River, showing the businesses along the east side of the river in 1901. Notice the numerous examples of advertising painted on the brick buildings—forerunners of today's billboards along expressways.

Pastime activities for the very young Elgin child consisted of tea parties for one's animals and, as in the case of this young lady, a stroll with a favorite teddy bear friend on wheels. This posed backyard scene was taken at Mable Adams's home at 428 Division Street at the turn of the 20th century.

A young lady might also go walking with the family dog and pose for the photographer in a pretty calico dress, topped off with an elaborate daisy-covered straw hat. This young girl beside the water pump does not seem very happy, nor does the dog, about this outing.

Another favorite pastime activity for Elginites of all ages was coasting on ice-covered, hilly city streets in the winter. Here we see a lively group of nine riding a coaster named "Dixie" on West Chicago Street in January of 1891. Additional pictures taken by this photographer, Galen Williams, show a larger coaster with 13 people on board!

The Lords Park upper lagoon gave ice skaters a real chance to show their stuff. Here is a group of young skaters involved in a race around a flagged course. The abundance of parks in Elgin added to the quality of life for the residents of the city all year long. While this picture is from a later time, it does depict the races from earlier times.

Elgin's own "Buster Brown" inspired the creation of a Buster Brown Bread Company. Here, employees prepare to join a parade, with their bread delivery wagons colorfully decked out with American flags and with a little boy dressed as Buster Brown ready to ride on top of the second wagon. The white spot to the right of Buster is a sun reflection off a piece of metal on the front wagon.

This photograph details a Fourth of July parade of the 1890s, and this seems to be the famous Elgin Watch Company Band. The hundreds of umbrellas are being carried by men and women. The umbrella tops are an artistic take-off of the American flag, with two red and three white stripes surrounded by all the stars in the flag.

94

Circuses such as Hagenbeck & Wallace often came to town. This magnificent horse-drawn wagon features a real steam calliope (KALL-ee-oap). The wagon was painted a bright primary color, with gold three-dimensional carvings. Art Eck captured the calliope in action on the corner of Bluff and Liberty in 1911. Start up some music on any normally quiet city street, and the children race to the source!

The entire downtown was decked out for an Elk's Street parade and gathering of the clan in 1902. Booths were set up on the street to sell wares. Buildings were emblazoned with 20-foot Elk banners, and tricolor bunting was placed on city light poles. The city cable cars sported banners advertising the day—August 28th.

Circuses and carnivals timed their trips to communities to coincide with other planned events whenever possible, in order to maximize their business. This carnival attraction, called "The Roman Coliseum," featured boxers, wrestlers, baton manipulators, and fencers. This 1902 image by Charles B. Todd shows, as a blur, the steady stream of customers entering the attraction.

Photographs of early carnival side shows, with sky-high canvas advertising mysteries to be found inside, are extremely rare. "The Great London Ghost Show" was on the corner of DuPage and Spring, and for one thin dime, you would be thrilled and frightened by stories involving garland-bearing angels combating skies filled with devils.

After the Chicago World's Fair in 1893, the iron monger Ferris's "wheel" became very popular. After a promoter on Coney Island failed to buy the original, he built his own and called it a Ferris wheel anyway. Amusement parks and side show operators all began to build their own versions of Ferris's ride. Photographer Todd must have had the operator stop the machinery of the 18-person ride, so he could get a good shot. The light streak to the right of the crowd appears to be fast moving children. This ride was located on River (Grove) at Chicago Street and was also from the 1902 carnival.

"Gentlemen, start your engines," was a phrase coined soon after the Duryea Motor Wagon Company made its first auto in 1896. Frank B. "Tootie" Wood, an auto enthusiast, proposed that Elgin host a road race. The circuit was 8.5 miles long. Thus was born the famous Elgin National Road Races, which took place from 1910 to 1920, except during the war years.

Pit crews stood ready to install Michelin batteries and tires. Other companies had crews ready to install auto products by Mercer, Cino, and Abbott. This remarkable photograph is of the 1911 races, when Len Zengle won in his National car averaging 66.5 mph. The track is filled with people who have come down to meet their favorite driver.

Postcards were sent all over the country advertising the races. This clever drawing pokes fun at the sport of auto racing with its use of a duck for a horn, a railroad locomotive cow catcher, and a coal-burning engine. The clever brake lever not only stops coal from entering the "engine," but also engages a front wheel brake!

Eddie Hearne is sitting at the wheel of his car No. 5, a chain-driven Fiat 70. The man in front of the car, with goggles and an armband, is Hearne's riding mechanic. Hearne suffered a bad wrist, so a driver named Hill tried to finish the race. The steering wheel had taped "knots" for a better grip. Unfortunately, the car dropped out at the 27th lap with a broken gear housing.

Auto racing greats such as Barney Oldfield and Ray Harroun ran in the Elgin National. Car manufacturers such as National, Benz, Simplex, Jackson, Fiat, and Marmon entered race cars. The races were held in August and drew huge crowds. This was an opportunity for "boys" to play with their "toys." This photograph captures that spirit and is titled "Ralph and Billy, Same old smile." The Ralph in the photograph was Ralph Mulford, who won the first Elgin National with a top speed of 62.5 m.p.h. and was awarded a first prize of $1,000. The Billy in the photograph was his mechanic in this race. The Elgin National in 1911 saw three racers killed, a collapsed grandstand that injured 50 people, and eight people hurt on the track. Another bloody crash happened in the 1914 race, when Spencer Wishart and his mechanic died. Their car shot into the air over some spectators and crashed into a tree. With spectators standing so close to the roadway, together with the speeds of the car, it is a wonder that there were not more deaths at these races.

While the adults were caught up in road race fever, Elgin's young boys set out to build their own version of race cars. Local junkyards and garbage cans yielded up a treasure trove of parts for the boys. Where do you find sturdy wheels? This in not a problem. The boys used coffee-grinder wheels, which were made from the rejects found in the Elgin Foundry.

In sporting goggles and caps, and with a serious look on their faces, these two drivers are in the final lap of the race. Car number 3, which has held the lead for the entire race, must now face the challenge from car number 4 on his left, which has the edge with its smaller and faster non-coffee-grinder wheels. Reaching speeds in excess of 10 m.p.h. at the last minute, car number 4 crosses the finish line in time to glare back at his losing combatant.

These pictures of boys racing were staged by photographer Galen Williams. The race was on Crystal Street, just north of South Street. The car was designed and built by Paul Carpenter, and the driver of this car was Jack Bodoff. This appears to be a motorless racer that depended on gravity to work. Coffee-grinder wheels also made great steering wheels!

Even better than building dream cars, young boys liked to pile into a real car and go for a spin once they finished a tough ball game at Camp Elgin. This nine-man squad is proudly sporting their gloves, bat, and catcher's chest protector. The tent shown in the background is large enough to sleep this entire team from 1906.

Coasters were not only found on icy Elgin streets. Another kind of coaster was available in Elgin. Eventually called roller coasters, because the cars were suspended on wheels fitted to tracks, Elgin boasted one of the longest and most thrilling rides for miles around. It was installed at Trout Park and mounted on a framework of wooden supports under the metal tracks.

A sculpture, in which children hold an umbrella while the fountain drops water over it, was installed in Lord's Park. This fountain provided a simple pleasure for simpler times. Note the bandstand to the right. On many a summer day, competing park bands might be heard serenading their audiences with the music of Sousa or Paull.

When a horseless buggy rolled out of the Moody Bros. Machine Shop at 56 River (now Grove), the brothers wanted to be photographed while they sat in their car. Victor Moody is the driver, and sitting next to him is Charles. Andrew and Axel are in the rear. The picture was taken in front of the Elgin Butter Company, *c.* 1903.

During the late Victorian period, spas sprang up all over the country, each claiming to have foods and exercise programs for what ailed you. Patent medicine was sold in drug stores. For centuries, mineral water had been called a cure-all. In this photograph, a car-load of young beauties stops for a drink from the mineral spring in Wing Park.

Eight

LOG CABINS, PAINTED LADIES, AND DECOMANIA

Elgin's older homes and buildings are like windows through which we can look to see the city's past. These structures are like the land itself, and they should be treasured, protected, and passed down to future generations intact. Elgin was transformed into a boom town once good transportation lines were established, and its dairy, printing, and watchmaking industries began to thrive. Workers flocked to the city, and they had to be housed. Elgin's many hotels were only temporary quarters for a growing residential population. Soon houses for many different social classes began to dot both sides of the river. While in the downtown area, architectural gems were razed to build higher and more modern structures. Residential homes and neighborhoods remained, for the most part, intact. Today, these historic neighborhoods tell the story of early Elgin and help us understand the people that lived out their lives in these dream homes of long ago.

Elgin's first architectural form was the log cabin, which served so many frontier settlers as their first home. The Gifford brothers were the first to build such permanent structures. Log cabins were soon replaced, and multi-roomed houses sprang up like mushrooms in Elgin. Housing for the working class tended to be simple, inexpensive, and built according to a common formula, like those of William Levitt that were built after World War II. Managers and owners of businesses and the wealthy could afford fancier structures in Elgin's high Victorian era. Today, many of these elaborate structures remain and have been restored to their original "Painted Lady" look. These huge, ostentatious structures, with their turrets and multitude of rooms with high ceilings, came under criticism at the turn of the century when a simpler style of architecture, with a less decorated exterior, emerged. It was called moderne, and its plain-jacketed buildings dominated the American landscape almost to the end of the century, when people began to demand some decoration on their buildings once more.

This view of Elgin, across the Fox River from the west bank, around 1873, shows the railroad engine house. A windmill is being utilized for running various types of machinery in the shop inside the structure.

When the Gifford brothers settled in Elgin in the mid-1830s, James T. built a cabin on the corner of what are now Prairie and Gifford Streets. His brother, Hezekiah, built the first cabin, which was 16 feet square. James T. Gifford's cabin was to become Elgin's first meetinghouse, for it served at various times as a meetinghouse, school, and church, as well as a family home.

The Kimball House was one of Elgin's earliest hotels. Other hotels in town at this time were the City Hotel, Waverly Hotel, Chicago House, and Western House. Some of the hotels had some architectural flair, such as the three-story, Mansard-roofed Western House. Others were no-nonsense, three-story brick structures, such as the Waverly House.

Shortly after the Civil War, home builders developed a more efficient way to mass produce housing. They became known as Balloon-Frame houses and were built with standard-size lumber. Many were constructed without an architect or professional carpenter. Here are David W. and Mary Graves Sharp, standing with young son Roy outside their nicely detailed cottage at 515 South Street in 1887.

Some of the balloon-frame cottages had elevated basements. Others, built on a hill, had walk-out basements. The rather plain cottage on the right stands in sharp contrast to the almost "painted lady" house on the left, with its fancy, high-Victorian roof edge and molded decorations at the peak of the roof and on the corners. A bicyclist has paused a moment to be included in this picture.

Pete Sharp is seated in the center of the photograph in front of his house on Villa Street. The dress of the family, its large number of members, and the house itself tell us that the Sharp family was solid middle class. Various family members are posed with croquet mallets. The house is full of gingerbread, fan-like details and has been painted with six different colors. This was a true "painted lady" house.

This home at 410 Jackson is a fine example of an Elgin mansion. This three-story structure, made of stone and shingle siding, combines many old architectural styles into one confusing "new style." Plain columns with Gothic, Dutch, Victorian, and Queen Anne elements, as well as curved real and fake porches, combine with a huge four-sided front roof to create a balanced and good-looking turn-of-the-century house.

This 1885 structure has a mansard shingled roof, punctuated with many round, capped, fancy, floor-to-ceiling windows. Fake banisters line the second floor and further create the illusion of an architectural frosted wedding cake. The house contained 16 rooms, and the outside stonework was said to have come from New York. This home at 349 Prairie, next to Gifford Park, was the site of many fashionable parties.

Ironwork fencing began to replace common wood fencing by the turn of the century. Originally, fencing in a frontier town was to keep one's animals from wandering away or to prevent other animals from wandering onto your land. This is the David C. Cook home at Gifford and Division, which later served as the Bowes Nursing Home.

Dr. Roy Wilcox, an Elgin dentist, captured his young wife in front of their home at 46 Enterprise Street in 1901. Mrs. Wilcox is dressed for the weather in leather gloves and a floor-length winter coat. Her blouse is collared with a bow tie, and her fancy, feathered hat is held in place by a long hat pin through her pulled-back hair. Ornate, spindled woodwork surrounds the porch, and the first-floor windows have stained glass at the top, complete with brackets and a shingled mini roof on one of the windows. The second-floor windows have shutters, and there is a wide, overhanging roof on the house. Fancy molding caps off the porch columns in this typical middle-class home in Elgin.

Buildings in downtown Elgin during the Victorian era were a mixture of older, simple, Fox Valley limestone structures and newer stores, which featured fancy towers and gables with saw-tooth molding along the upper roof line. The use of ornamental tin sheeting was to be found on the outside of stores as decorative panels and on the inside of stores as ceiling decorations. Fancy, shipped-in, red brick was used on some buildings, and the city of Elgin even allowed merchants to build iron porches over the wide sidewalks in town. The use of cheap ceramic tiles for exterior decoration came into style at the turn of the century. In this block of old Elgin, there is Zook's Bookseller, a barber shop, and the Kelley Hotel. The hotel sports modern, lighted hotel and cafe signs.

PROFESSIONAL BUILDING,
ELGIN, ILL.—26

The first skyscrapers were made possible by the use of an iron skeleton for the outer walls, instead of 6-foot-thick supporting stonework. Later use of steel for the skeleton of buildings made even higher structures possible. The eight-story Professional Building at 164 Division Street uses an inner structure with cast concrete. This is an example of the style called new-Gothic.

Detailing around the windows is quite spectacular and is found all the way up the front of the Professional Building. Many Chicago-school architects had stopped ornamenting their skyscrapers past the first few floors due to the expense and to the fact that the details could not be seen well from the sidewalk. (JME.)

What a difference a year made in Elgin commercial architecture! Modern, simplistic, German-styled architecture began to take hold in America and Elgin. Take off all the decorative "noodles" of past houses and commercial buildings, and what you have is not pseudo-Greek temples, but Post cereal box skyscrapers and houses. Streamlined, but with curves, was the new watchword, not only of architecture but also in clothing, trains, radios, and compacts. Plastic and chrome were the new materials of the Art Deco period. Elgin's architectural beacon, the Tower Building, was constructed in 1929 for the Home Bank. Although the building is Deco in character, it does incorporate a limited amount of decoration so as not to completely shock traditional Elginites. After all, are banks not supposed to be conservative and non–risk takers?

George and Mary Lord bought 50 acres for $16,000 and gave them to the city for a park. A pavilion was built in 1896 but had to be rebuilt in 1898 after it burned. This wonderful park also had a zoo that housed bears, monkeys, peacocks, bison, elk, deer, and a lion named Lord Spark.

Our last look at architecture in Elgin takes quite a different twist, with this view of farm silos. Structures such as these are found all around Elgin and throughout the entire nation. The next time you pass an old, steel-ribbed silo in this area, chances are it was manufactured by the Elgin firm of Mason and Lawrence, and assembled by the local farmer. The silo to the right has an internal steel skeleton for strength. (JME.)

Nine

CALL TO ARMS AND OTHER DISASTERS

Elgin's Company E, a National Guard unit, had a hard time in the 19th century. They were often called out to help the fire and police departments or to serve as strike-breakers, especially in the LaSalle coal strike riot and the Pullman Railroad Strike of 1894. Elgin soldiers saw duty in the Spanish-American War and also became involved in the Civil War. When not putting down riots and fighting in wars, the Company E played at war two weeks each summer, staging fake battles. On the real battlefield, Elgin's young men faced various diseases, which killed as many, or more, than the enemy's bullets.

Disaster was spelled with a capital "D" in early Elgin. The forces of nature were responsible for some of these catastrophes. Several times, the Fox River raged, taking bridges with it. By the 1880s, Elgin had lost five bridges. Cyclones hit Elgin, ripping out trees and tearing up buildings. The city's fire department was kept busy, quelling fires and trying to keep flames from spreading to other buildings. Carpenters were busy building patrol wagons to deal with crimes, including brawls that started in the taverns.

All in all, Elgin was a normal city during the beginning of the industrial age. With all the growth, there would be problems unheard of in former days, when almost all Americans were self-sufficient farmers, and the nearest village was far away.

This is a view looking across the Fox River to the east side of Elgin in 1902. In this city of churches, count the spires from left to right: First Congregational, First Baptist, St. Mary's, and Bethlehem Lutheran Churches.

Seth Green, Elgin's first police officer, was elected as constable and justice of the peace in 1836. The holders of this office changed annually until 1870, when John (Jack) Powers was appointed. Elgin's first patrol wagon was built by Henry Plummer, a local carpenter, for the police department in 1891.

Volunteers manned the first fire department in 1877. The firemen of a more modern Department 5 are showing off their shiny new fire wagon with ladders in front of the station. Notice the spokes on these wagon wheels.

116

The first bridge was built in 1837 but was carried off in 1849. Another wooden bridge was constructed, which lasted until 1866, when it was removed and an iron bridge built in its place. This structure collapsed when a herd of cattle was driven over it! Yet another bridge was constructed, but it too collapsed in 1869. This one was replaced by an iron structure that was destroyed by ice and flood in 1881. At the time, such occurrences were common.

In Loving Remembrance of

Arthur Elmer Peterson
Died May 30, 1901.
Age 6 yrs, 10 days.

Gone but not forgotten

Precious darling, he has left us,
Left us, yes, for evermore;
But we hope to meet our loved one
On that bright and happy shore.
Lonely the house and sad the hours
Since our dear one has gone;
But oh! a brighter home than ours
In Heaven is now his own.

The death of children was common at the turn of the century, but it was still a tragedy for those who knew the child. This Fox Valley child was remembered by family and friends with this funeral card, but the death was not recorded in the area newspapers.

The fire department was kept busy in a large downtown filled with buildings with connecting walls. These hose companies are busy cooling off the remains of an unidentified fire. All that was left standing were the iron ceiling supports, with piles of charred wood and ashes on the ground.

Cyrus H. Woodruff brought a foundry to Elgin in 1879. By their very nature, foundries are vulnerable to fire. The foundry and machine shop were destroyed by fire in 1891 and again in 1917. This photograph was taken after the 1917 fire.

The stand pipe for Elgin's water works at Spring and Cooper collapsed at 7:35 in the morning of March 14, 1900, releasing a rush of water. This tank had a capacity of 525,000 gallons and was practically full at the time. Heavy ice was blamed for the fall. Because the ground slopes toward the river at that point, the nearby houses were not damaged.

The first of three twisters to hit Elgin blew in on May 25, 1896. This cyclone hit the south side of the city. There was much damage, but no lives were lost in this storm. The hardest-hit business was the Elgin Sewing Machine and Bicycle Company on the southeast side.

The 1896 cyclone hit the asylum for the insane, then crossed the river, uprooting trees and outhouses in its path. The roof and part of the chimney of this house were taken away, but plenty of people came over to help neighbors in need.

When the next cyclone hit in March 1920, residents were not quite so lucky. Although this one also began in the southwest part of town, it turned and ran through the business district, cutting a swath about 200 yards wide. Two people were killed at the Grand Theater, shown here.

Both the First Congregational and First Baptist Churches were badly damaged, and lives were lost at each—three at the First Congregational and one at the First Baptist. The cyclone hit after services were over, thus limiting the loss, but about 30 people were seriously injured.

Trees were ripped apart as the cyclone continued on its way. A person in a home on Adams Street was the seventh casualty of this disaster. These houses seem to have escaped damage, but about 25 homes were destroyed.

It stormed and snowed most of the month of March in 1881. Milk trains were interrupted, and milk became scarce in Chicago. The *Elgin Advocate* reported that the snow was up to the top of the engines. Trains were snowbound for two weeks, and rail travel was difficult until April 15th, when a heavy rain started that melted the snow.

At times, the snow was 6 feet deep on the downtown streets. Snow was removed from the boardwalks, and teams hauled it away as fast as possible. A local photographer, John Manley Adams, recorded the scenes, lest we forget.

Coal miners were rioting in LaSalle, Illinois, in May of 1894, and Elgin's Company E was among those 500 guardsmen called to restore peace. The men from Elgin arrived on May 25th to help liberate the prisoners taken on May 24th. By the 29th, all was quiet, and the National Guard left LaSalle on May 31st. Two months later, they served in the railroad strike.

Company E of the Third Regiment was organized in Elgin on September 23, 1877, with 55 officers and men. They trained regularly during the year and spent two weeks in camp each summer. Two years after the strike involvement, Company E was able to enjoy a more normal time at summer camp. Entertaining the troops are, from left to right, Bob Barnes, William Gieske, C. Fred Gieske, and George Foster.

123

This portrait is of Louis P. Andrews, a veteran of the Spanish-American War. Company F of the 25th U.S. Infantry, the black regiment, was praised for its part in the heavy fighting before Santiago. The Third Illinois also served in Puerto Rico. Newton, a local photographer, took pictures of many Spanish-American War veterans.

Fred Starring posed for this portrait in October of 1861. Elgin provided many soldiers for the Civil War: one company each to the 7th Illinois in April 1861; to the 36th Illinois Volunteers in July of 1861; to the 52nd in September 1861; to the 55th in October 1861; to the 58th in 1862; to the 69th in June 1862; to the 127th in September 1862; and to the Elgin Battery in November 1862.

Company E, Third Infantry Regiment of the Illinois National Guard was headquartered in Elgin from 1882 until it was federalized in 1917. In August of 1898, this unit served in Puerto Rico during the Spanish-American War. The men saw little action, but most United States soldiers were hit hard with malaria and typhoid fever while there. They were brought home in November of that year.

In 1909, the National Guard encampment was held at Wing Park. It was named Camp Deneen, for the governor of Illinois, for the duration of the camp. The balloon section was attached to the signal corp. They used this "Chicago" balloon in connection with field maneuvers. The balloon was as tall as a 13-story building and held 110,000 cubic feet of gas.

The First Cavalry under Colonel Milton J. Foreman was 700 strong. Troops from Peoria, Springfield, and Macomb met the Chicago troops and, after parading through Chicago, marched overland to Elgin, stopping a mile west of Addison for the night. Elginites visited the camp to view the horses and watch drills and a mock battle.

Index